Alligators and Other Crocodilians

By the same author

The Emperor's New Clothes
Snakes
What Do Animals Eat?

Alligators
and Other
Crocodilians

BY RUTH BELOV GROSS

Four Winds Press   New York

Library of Congress Cataloging in Publication Data

Gross, Ruth Belov.
    Alligators and other crocodilians.

    SUMMARY: Discusses the crocodilian family which is
composed of four animals: alligator, crocodile, caiman,
and gavial.
    1. Crocodilia — Juvenile literature. [1. Crocodilia]
I. Title.
QL666.C9G76   1978   598.1'4   77–18310
ISBN 0–590–07556–X

Published by Four Winds Press
A Division of Scholastic Magazines, Inc., New York, N.Y.
Copyright © 1976 by Ruth Belov Gross
Printed in the United States of America
Library of Congress Catalog Card Number: 77–18310
1   2   3   4   5   82   81   80   79   78

Photo Credits

Arthur W. Ambler/National Audubon Society/Photo Researchers, p. 41; Annan Photo Features, pp. 25, 31; Hugh B. Cott, p. 21; Treat Davidson/National Audubon Society/Photo Researchers, p. 10; F. Erize/Bruce Coleman, pp. 4, 13 bottom; Lew Field/Photo Researchers, p. 12; Florida News Bureau, p. 43; Leslie D. Garrick, p. 7 top; Andy Koukoulis, p. 7 bottom; Leszczynski/Animals Animals, p. 36; Les Line/National Audubon Society/Photo Researchers, p. 13 top; Tom McHugh/Photo Researchers, Inc., p. 9; Norman Myers/Bruce Coleman, p. 47; National Zoological Park/Smithsonian Institution, p. 29; Wilfred T. Neill, pp. 24, 33, 39; R. R. Pawlowski/Bruce Coleman, pp. 15, 22-23; Bucky & Avis Reeves/Photo Researchers, p. 5; Leonard Lee Rue III/Bruce Coleman, p. 3; Leonard Lee Rue III/National Audubon Society/Photo Researchers, pp. vi, 52; Leonard Lee Rue IV/Bruce Coleman, p. 27; J. R. Simon/Photo Trends, p. 19; Frederick Kent Truslow, jacket, pp. 16, 32, 38; Wide World Photos, p. 51; Ylla/Photo Researchers, p. 35.

For the boys and girls at P.S. 80 and P.S. 183 in Manhattan and at the Polk Street School in Franklin Square, New York, who asked me questions about alligators and other crocodilians when I was writing this book.

And with my thanks to Peter Brazaitis, Superintendent, Department of Herpetology, New York Zoological Park, Bronx, New York, who helped me make sure that my answers were right.

Alligator

This book is about alligators and crocodiles. It is also about their relatives, the caimans and the gavials.

Alligators are famous. So are crocodiles. Everybody knows about them.

Caimans and gavials are not so famous. Many people have never even heard of them.

All four are very much alike, though.

When people say *alligator*, they usually mean the kind in this picture — the American alligator. It lives in the southeastern part of the United States.

American alligators grow to be two or three meters* long. Some are even longer. If you had an alligator three meters long lying on your bed, most of its tail would hang over the end.

There is only one other kind of alligator in the world. It lives in China.

The most famous kind of crocodile is the Nile crocodile, the one in the picture.

Nile crocodiles live in Africa. Many of them grow to be four to six meters** long.

*Three meters are about ten feet.

**about 13 to 20 feet

Crocodile

Caimans live in Central America and South America. Most kinds of caimans are not much more than two meters* long.

*Two meters are about six and a half feet.

Caiman (**kay**-*mun*)

*Gavial (**gay**-vee-al)*

There is only one kind of gavial. It lives in India and other parts of southern Asia.

Gavials are big. Some are more than four and a half meters* long.

*about 15 feet

5

There is one word that scientists use a lot when they talk about alligators, crocodiles, caimans, and gavials. The word is *crocodilian* (crock-uh-**dill**-yun).

It can mean an alligator.

It can mean a crocodile.

It can mean a caiman.

It can mean a gavial.

It cannot mean any other kind of animal.

All crocodilians are reptiles. All crocodilians have long snouts, long tails, four short legs, tough skin, and sharp teeth.

They all live in places that are warm all year round. And they all spend part of their time in the water and part of their time on land.

Almost all crocodilians grow to be very big. The very biggest are more than six meters* long — longer than a big car.

Many people think a crocodilian looks cute when it's small — but not when it's grown.

*about 20 feet

Baby alligator

Grown alligator

7

Millions and millions of years ago, there were more than a hundred different kinds of crocodilians. Their closest relatives were the dinosaurs.

About 70 million years ago, the dinosaurs died out. Most of the crocodilians died out too. But a few kinds of crocodilians did not die out. They kept on having babies.

The crocodilian babies grew up and had babies of their own. Then the babies grew up and had babies. This kept going on and on and on — and is still going on today.

Today there are two kinds of alligators, 13 or 14 kinds of crocodiles, seven or eight kinds of caimans, and one kind of gavial.

The best place to see a crocodilian is in a zoo. When you go to the zoo, how can you tell which crocodilian is which?

You'll know a gavial when you see one. Gavials have the longest snouts and the most teeth.

But there are not many gavials in zoos — or even in the world.

The other crocodilians are harder to tell apart.

Some people say you can tell an alligator from a crocodile by the shape of its snout. They say an alligator's snout is wider. But this only works for American alligators and American crocodiles.

There's another way to tell the difference. Look at the teeth.

An American crocodile is on the top.
An American alligator is on the bottom.

extra-big bottom tooth

Crocodile

When a crocodile's mouth is closed, you can still see a lot of teeth — especially an extra-big bottom tooth sticking up near the front.

But you won't see an alligator's bottom teeth when its mouth is closed. You won't see a caiman's bottom teeth either.

Alligator

Caiman

13

Zoo keepers say that crocodiles move faster than alligators. They say that crocodiles have nastier tempers too.

Don't feel bad if you can't tell what kind of crocodilian you are looking at. Most people can't. You can always ask the zoo keeper. Or you can read the sign.

How do scientists know which crocodilian is which?

They know that some kinds of crocodilians are bigger, or darker, or smoother, than other kinds.

They know that some kinds have more teeth or smaller feet or wider snouts.

They look for differences like these.

Sometimes, when scientists go to a place where crocodilians live, they do not know what kind of crocodilians they will find. So they measure and count, they draw pictures, they take photographs, and they write down everything they see and hear. Some day, scientists might discover a new kind of crocodilian this way.

Saltwater crocodile

The biggest kind of crocodilian in the world lives in India and southeast Asia and in Australia — and on many islands in between. It is called the saltwater crocodile.

A saltwater crocodile can grow to be about seven and a half meters* long — or longer.

No matter how big a crocodilian is, it was very, very small to begin with. It came from an egg that wasn't much bigger than the eggs you eat.

*about 25 feet

This is a male alligator and a female alligator after they have mated. Crocodilians mate in shallow water.

Before a mother crocodilian can lay eggs, she must mate with a male crocodilian. Later she will make a nest for her eggs.

Some kinds of crocodilians make their nests by digging a hole in the ground. Other kinds make their nests by piling up grass and mud and anything else that is handy — leaves, stems, twigs, branches.

Alligators always make piled-up nests. A mother alligator uses her hind feet to shovel everything in a heap. She packs the nest down by crawling all over it, and she makes it round by pushing against it.

At the top of the nest, the mother alligator scoops out a space for the eggs. She lays about 40 to 60 eggs in this scooped-out place. Then she gently pushes mud and grass over the eggs.

The nest is about as high as a dining-room table. It is as big around as an open umbrella — a big umbrella.

A mother alligator usually lies on her nest. That is how she guards it. As long as she is near the nest, her eggs are safe.

She might stay near the nest until the eggs are ready to hatch — about two months. Or she might leave her nest after a few weeks. If she leaves, some enemy is likely to come along and eat the eggs. In Florida, the enemy could be a raccoon or a skunk.

Mother alligator lying on her nest

Nile crocodile mothers always make their nests by digging a hole. After the mother crocodile lays her eggs, she fills up the hole with sand. She smooths out the sand with her body, and then she lies right on top of the nest.

In Africa, where Nile crocodiles live, there are big hungry lizards and big birds and baboons and hyenas. They would dig up the crocodile eggs and eat them if they had a chance. But a Nile crocodile mother hardly ever gives them a chance.

Nile crocodiles lay 25, 50, or sometimes 95 eggs at a time. Most of the eggs will hatch in about three months. Some will never hatch at all.

Nile crocodile mother lying on her nest

Where is the father crocodile? The father is not around. He wandered away after he mated with the mother.

Alligator fathers do the same thing.

*This little crocodile is
starting to come out of its egg.*

At last the eggs are ready to hatch.

Inside the eggs, the baby crocodilians are making soft grunting noises. And they are rubbing their snouts against the shells.

Each baby has a tiny sharp bump on the tip of its snout. As the baby rubs its head back and forth, the bump makes a slit in the shell. The baby pokes its snout through the slit — and then comes all the way out.

Can the babies get out of the nest by themselves? Scientists don't

The crocodile has hatched.
It is called a hatchling now.

agree. Most scientists think the mother has to open the nest and let the babies out.

A crocodile hatchling weighs just a little more than a candy bar. It is about 28 centimeters* long. The hatchling can run around right away, and it can swim and climb and jump.

How did such a big hatchling ever fit inside an egg that was only seven or eight centimeters** long? The hatchling was all curled up in the egg! It uncurled itself when it came out.

*about 11 inches

**about three inches

This is an alligator hatchling.
It is grayish-black and has yellowish stripes.
The stripes will fade away in a few years.

As soon as the hatchlings get out of the nest, they head for the water. Nobody has figured out how they know where the water is. But they go straight to it.

At first, the hatchlings stay around the water's edge. It is the safest place for them to be. The stripes on their bodies make them look like the weeds and reeds that grow near the water.

If some enemy — maybe a big frog or a big hungry bird — comes after them, they can jump in the water and hide. Only their eyes and the tips of their snouts will show.

24

These two little caimans are hiding in the water.

What if a big bird does grab a baby alligator? The baby alligator will cry out. It will go *yonk, yonk* — over and over, in a loud, high voice. That won't stop the big bird. It will go ahead and eat the little alligator.

But if an adult alligator is around, it will come to the baby. It will hiss and growl and chase the bird away.

Adult crocodilians often help baby crocodilians this way.

When a crocodilian is a few years old, it leaves its weedy hiding place. Now it will go where the water is deeper. And for the rest of its life it can be found in some watery place — a lake or a river, a pond or a marsh, a swamp or a creek or a ditch.

Crocodilians get big very fast.

By the time an alligator or a Nile crocodile is six or seven years old, it is about two meters* long.

Its baby stripes have faded away, and it has stopped making baby noises. It can roar and growl and bellow now, and it can hiss louder than it did when it was small. It is starting to be a grown-up crocodilian.

From now on, it will grow very slowly — not more than four or five centimeters** a year.

Many six-year-old alligators are old enough to mate and have babies. Nile crocodiles do not mate until they are about 20 years old.

*about six and a half feet

**about one and a half or two inches

Biggy, a saltwater crocodile, lived in the National Zoo in Washington, D.C., until he died in 1974. He was about 57 years old – probably the oldest zoo crocodilian in the world. He was certainly the biggest. He weighed almost a ton, and he was about five meters long. (Five meters are about sixteen and a half feet.)

How long do crocodilians live?

If anybody tells you that crocodilians can live for 200 or 300 years — don't believe it!

Most scientists think a crocodilian can live for only 50 to 75 years. Others think that 100 years might be right, but they can't prove it.

Crocodilians are good swimmers. They swish their tails from side to side to push themselves ahead.

The faster they swish their tails, the faster they move in the water. Mostly, though, they just float.

When a crocodilian is in the water, it is very hard to see. Most crocodiles and caimans and gavials are brownish-green. Grown alligators are grayish-black. They are almost the color of the water they swim in.

Sometimes all you can see is a crocodilian's back and snout. It looks like a log that way.

Sometimes only its snout sticks out of the water. It must have its snout out to breathe. But a crocodilian can stay underwater for as long as an hour. It holds its breath the whole time.

A crocodilian has everything on its snout that it needs for seeing, hearing, breathing, and smelling.

When a crocodilian goes under the water, it doesn't get water up its nose or in its ears or in its eyes.

Special muscles close its nose.

Special muscles close its ears.

And special eyelids — like clear window shades — slide across its eyes.

The flaps in this alligator's throat are open. They will shut tight when the alligator dives under the water.

A crocodilian doesn't get water down its throat, either. It has special flaps in its throat that keep the water out. The flaps close tight when the crocodilian dives.

Sea water is too salty for most kinds of crocodilians. But it is just right for saltwater crocodiles. The only place they live is in the sea or in salty waters near the sea.

*The water is really a crocodilian's home. If the water dries up,
a crocodilian will walk on dry land until it finds water again.
This is an American alligator.*

You can live where it is very hot or very cold. Crocodilians cannot. A crocodilian must always be in a place that is warm — about as warm as a kitchen when someone is cooking.

The temperature of your body always stays about the same, no matter where you are. But a crocodilian's temperature goes up when it is in a hot place and down when it is in a cold place. If its body temperature goes up too high or down too low, the crocodilian dies.

The days are nice and warm in the places where crocodilians live. So in the daytime the crocodilians can lie around on the land — and maybe take a nap.

At night the land grows cool. The water will be warmer than the land. So at night the crocodilians keep their bodies warm by going into the water.

Alligators lying in the warm sun

This alligator is lying partly on the land and partly in the water.
It is keeping warm and getting cool at the same time.

Sometimes the days get terribly hot — too hot for a crocodilian. On a day like that, an alligator or a crocodile might lie in the shade. Or it might cool off in the water for a while.

Scientists used to say that crocodilians and other reptiles were *cold-blooded.* That term is still used sometimes. But now most scientists use another word — *poikilothermic* (poy-kill-oh-**therm**-ick).

36

Crocodilians find most of their food in the water. They eat mostly at night. And mostly they eat fish.

But a crocodilian will eat just about any animal it can catch —

a bird that is skimming over the water,

a turtle that is swimming under the water,

a frog that is sitting on a lily pad,

a raccoon that is drinking at the water's edge.

A crocodilian will also eat animals that are already dead. It doesn't eat plants — unless it happens to swallow a lily pad along with a frog.

Once in a while in a zoo, an adult crocodilian will eat a baby crocodilian.

An alligator can crunch right through a turtle shell.

Crocodilians catch their food in some very sneaky ways.

Sometimes a crocodilian lies under the water. It keeps its mouth open and waits. When a fish or a turtle swims by — whamp! That's the end of the fish or the turtle.

Sometimes a crocodilian swims around with its snout sticking out. Suppose a pig is getting a drink at the water's edge. The crocodilian quickly dives under the water and swims straight to the pig.

When the crocodilian gets close to the pig, it lifts its snout out of the water — and grabs the pig in its jaws.

A crocodilian's jaws snap shut so hard that the strongest man in the world could not make them open up again. Its teeth are so sharp that they can jab straight through a slippery fish or a wiggly pig.

This tooth came from an alligator. Alligators, crocodiles, and caimans have 66 to 80 teeth. Gavials have more than 100! Whenever a tooth falls out, a new tooth grows in.

Crocodilians do not eat their food underwater. They bring it up to the top and eat it there. They swallow it in one gulp, without chewing it.

If an animal is too big to be swallowed in one gulp, a crocodilian will tear it in pieces. Then it will eat the pieces.

A young crocodilian eats small animals — tadpoles, small fish, small frogs, and maybe some dragonflies or water bugs or snails.

When it is older and bigger, it will catch bigger fish and other big animals — dogs or sheep or even a cow.

Gavials mostly eat fish, no matter how old and big they get. So as a gavial grows bigger, it just eats bigger fish.

A gavial's long, narrow snout is just the right shape for catching fish.

Sometimes a crocodilian won't eat at all when it is put in a zoo. Crocodilians can live for a long time without eating — three or four months at least.

In a zoo, the crocodilians usually get fed two or three times a week. They get fish and meat and rats and mice to eat. They almost always get vitamins too.

One alligator farm in Florida gave marshmallows to its alligators — just for fun. The alligators learned to like marshmallows so much that they began jumping out of the water to get them.

Do crocodilians eat people? Sometimes they do.

Every now and then, a saltwater crocodile or a Nile crocodile or a big American alligator will grab a person who is swimming. Or it might grab a person who has fallen out of a boat.

Mostly, though, crocodilians stay away from people.

A long time ago, people thought that alligators and crocodiles cried after they ate a human being. Nowadays we know this isn't true. But we still talk about crocodile tears.

We say that somebody is crying *crocodile tears* when he or she pretends to be sorry, but isn't really sorry at all.

This alligator is having a marshmallow snack.

All crocodilians eat stones. When they can't find stones, they eat pebbles or gravel or bits of wood or other hard things.

The stones and other hard things are not like regular food. They stay inside a crocodilian's stomach.

Scientists have different ideas about why crocodilians eat stones.

Some scientists think that crocodilians need stones in their stomachs to help them grind up their food.

Some scientists think that the stones keep a crocodilian from feeling hungry.

Some scientists think that stones make a crocodilian swim and dive better, because of the extra weight.

Adult crocodilians don't have many enemies. There are very few animals in the world that are big enough and strong enough to hurt them.

Every now and then, a lion or an elephant or a hippopotamus might kill a large Nile crocodile in Africa. A tiger might kill a crocodile in India. A jaguar or an anaconda might kill a caiman in South America. That's about all.

Human beings are the real enemies of crocodilians. Anybody with a gun can easily kill a big alligator or crocodile.

A crocodilian can always tell when an enemy is around. It can smell the enemy's smell, and it can hear the noise the enemy makes. Sometimes it sees the enemy coming.

A crocodilian rushes to the water when an enemy is coming. It doesn't walk. It runs! If it is already in the water, it dives to the bottom and stays there.

Do crocodilians fight with each other? Yes, but probably not very often.

When a crocodilian fights, it uses its strong jaws and sharp teeth. It can also give a good hard whack with its tail when it is swinging its body around.

On the river banks where Nile crocodiles spend their days, there are many kinds of birds. Some people call them crocodile-birds, because they are always hopping around the crocodiles.

The birds eat flies and leeches (a kind of worm) that they find on the crocodiles' skin and in their mouths. The birds get a good meal — and the crocodiles get rid of flies and leeches.

Sometimes an enemy frightens the birds. They scream and fly away suddenly. When the birds scream and fly away, the crocodiles rush to the water. By making a lot of noise and flying away, the birds may be giving the crocodiles an extra warning of danger.

There is a special word that scientists use when they talk about animals that are helpful to each other. The word is *symbiosis* (sim-by-**oh**-sis).

*The big crocodiles and the little birds
are useful to each other.*

In most parts of the world, there are not as many alligators, crocodiles, caimans, and gavials as there used to be.

What has happened to them?

Many crocodilians have died because people dried up the swamps and marshes where the crocodilians lived. The people wanted the land for houses and farms and roads.

Some crocodilians have been killed by people who were afraid of them — or who were angry because the crocodilians tore holes in their fishing nets.

Most of all, people have been shooting crocodilians to get their strong, smooth, leathery skins. The skins are made into shoes and belts and wallets. Then the shoes and belts and wallets are sold for a lot of money.

A man has just killed this alligator. Its skin will be made into shoes and other things.

Some people do not care if the crocodilians die out. They say, "So what? Who needs alligators and crocodiles anyway?"

We need them! Other animals need them too.

Some crocodilians eat small water animals that are the enemies of baby fish.

Other crocodilians help keep water plants alive. The waste that comes out of their bodies is fertilizer for the plants. Fish need these plants for food.

You could write a whole book about all the ways that crocodilians help living things.

Here is just one more way:

In the United States, there is a swampy place in Florida called the Everglades. Alligators live there, and so do frogs and turtles, fish and snakes, insects and birds, snails and crayfish, otters and raccoons.

There is not much rain in the Everglades in the winter. Many of the animals die. They cannot live without water.

But alligators are good at finding water. There is water deep in the ground. And when the dry season comes, the alligators start to dig down into the earth.

The alligators dig and dig, until at last they get to the water. Soon water fills the holes they have made, the way water fills the holes that people dig at the beach.

Some alligator holes are big enough for several alligators to live in.

The holes are like little ponds now. The alligators have a place to live for the winter. And without knowing it, they have saved other animals from dying. The water in the holes will keep thousands of animals alive until the rainy months come again.

It would be sad if we let the crocodilians die out.

Scientists would never be able to find out the things they still want to know about crocodilians.

Nobody would ever see another alligator, crocodile, caiman, or gavial anywhere — in a swamp or a lake or a pond, or even in a zoo. The closest relatives of the dinosaurs would be gone forever.

The striped places on this map show where crocodilians live.

Alligators live in the southeastern part of the United States and in China.

Four kinds of crocodiles live in Africa. Other kinds live in South America, Central America, and North America (including Mexico, Cuba, the West Indies, and a small part of Florida). There are crocodiles in Asia and Australia too.

Caimans live in Central America and South America.

Gavials live in India and other parts of southern Asia.

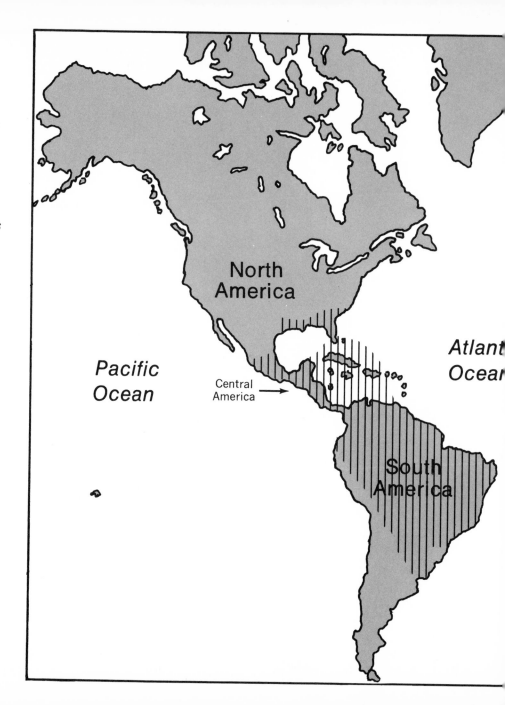

North America

Pacific Ocean

Central America

Atlant Ocea

South America

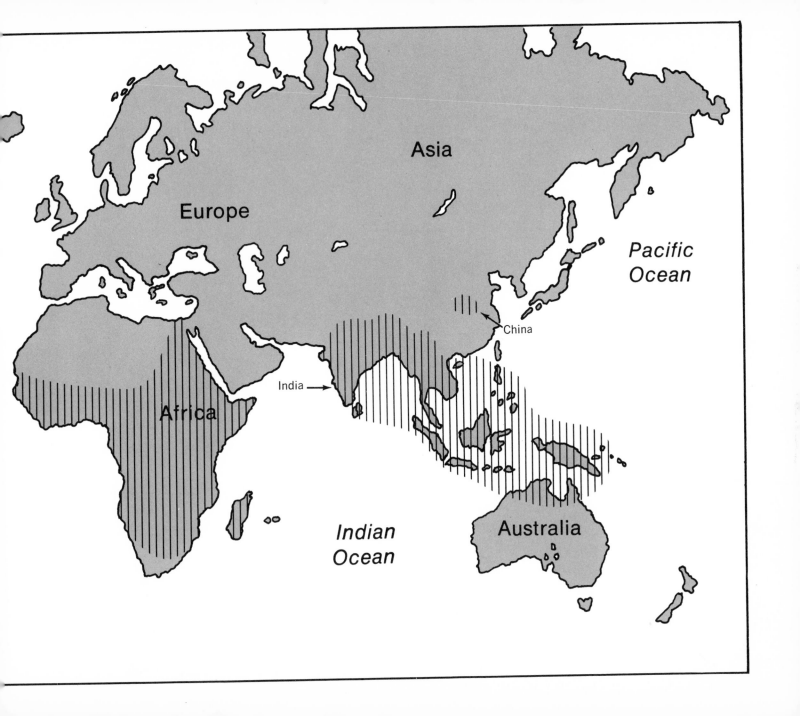

Europe

Asia

Africa

India →

China

Australia

Pacific
Ocean

Indian
Ocean

Index

If you are very interested in alligators and other crocodilians, you may want to be a *herpetologist* some day.

Herpetologists are scientists who study reptiles (crocodilians, snakes, lizards, and turtles) and amphibians (salamanders, frogs, and toads).